Questions lovingly answered by:

_______________ & _______________

How do I love thee? Let me count the ways.
I love thee to the depth and breadth and height
My soul can reach, when feeling out of sight
For the ends of being and ideal grace.
I love thee to the level of every day's
Most quiet need, by sun and candle-light.
I love thee freely, as men strive for right.
I love thee purely, as they turn from praise.
I love thee with the passion put to use
In my old griefs, and with my childhood's faith.
I love thee with a love I seemed to lose
With my lost saints. I love thee with the breath,
Smiles, tears, of all my life; and, if God choose,
I shall but love thee better after death.

- Elizabeth Barrett Browning -

Which way does the toilet paper roll go? Over or under?

☐ HER REPLY ☐ HIS REPLY

☐ HIS REPLY ☐ HER REPLY

What is one thing that frustrates you and what is the one thing you would really like to do to stop it?

☐ HER REPLY ☐ HIS REPLY

☐ HIS REPLY ☐ HER REPLY

How would you describe the feeling of being under attack?

☐ HER REPLY ☐ HIS REPLY

☐ HIS REPLY ☐ HER REPLY

What is the most important thing you've learned about yourself at this point in your life?

☐ HER REPLY ☐ HIS REPLY

☐ HIS REPLY ☐ HER REPLY

What kind of identity have you felt yourself?

☐ HER REPLY ☐ HIS REPLY

☐ HIS REPLY ☐ HER REPLY

What is the one thing you never do?

☐ HER REPLY ☐ HIS REPLY

☐ HIS REPLY ☐ HER REPLY

Are you good at getting your own way? Why or why not?

☐HER REPLY ☐HIS REPLY

☐HIS REPLY ☐HER REPLY

Have you ever been fired by your teacher?

☐HER REPLY ☐HIS REPLY

☐HIS REPLY ☐HER REPLY

What if you ran into a talking animal, what would you ask it? How would you react?

☐ HER REPLY ☐ HIS REPLY   ☐ HIS REPLY ☐ HER REPLY

If you could spend a lifetime in a city, where would you live?

☐ HER REPLY ☐ HIS REPLY   ☐ HIS REPLY ☐ HER REPLY

What are your interests?

☐ HER REPLY ☐ HIS REPLY

☐ HIS REPLY ☐ HER REPLY

Do you like to watch television? Why?

☐ HER REPLY ☐ HIS REPLY

☐ HIS REPLY ☐ HER REPLY

What causes you to think differently than most people?

☐ HER REPLY ☐ HIS REPLY

☐ HIS REPLY ☐ HER REPLY

What's your favorite TV show?

☐ HER REPLY ☐ HIS REPLY

☐ HIS REPLY ☐ HER REPLY

Are you a romantic or are you an idealist?

☐ HER REPLY ☐ HIS REPLY

☐ HIS REPLY ☐ HER REPLY

Who can you spend a whole day without being bored?

☐ HER REPLY ☐ HIS REPLY

☐ HIS REPLY ☐ HER REPLY

List of things that will work better together

Say something about your character that you wish you were more popular

If you had to choose a random moment in your life that has been the most remarkable what would that be and why?

☐ HER REPLY ☐ HIS REPLY

☐ HIS REPLY ☐ HER REPLY

How long has it been since you've gotten your nails done?

☐ HER REPLY ☐ HIS REPLY

☐ HIS REPLY ☐ HER REPLY

When was the last time you felt a sense of urgency to make sure everything was working?

☐ HER REPLY ☐ HIS REPLY

☐ HIS REPLY ☐ HER REPLY

How do you feel when you want something very badly and you cannot have it? Why is this so important to have?

☐ HER REPLY ☐ HIS REPLY

☐ HIS REPLY ☐ HER REPLY

Can you tell us about the people that make the music?

☐ HER REPLY ☐ HIS REPLY

☐ HIS REPLY ☐ HER REPLY

What is one thing that you would like to see more of from your time in the future?

☐ HER REPLY ☐ HIS REPLY

☐ HIS REPLY ☐ HER REPLY

How do you deal with the fact that this is an experiment?

☐ HER REPLY ☐ HIS REPLY

☐ HIS REPLY ☐ HER REPLY

What is one thing that you like most about yourself?

☐ HER REPLY ☐ HIS REPLY

☐ HIS REPLY ☐ HER REPLY

What was your first pet? Why did you choose this pet?

☐ HER REPLY ☐ HIS REPLY

☐ HIS REPLY ☐ HER REPLY

What causes you to become a good writer?

☐ HER REPLY ☐ HIS REPLY

☐ HIS REPLY ☐ HER REPLY

What did you like best about your job?

☐ HER REPLY ☐ HIS REPLY

☐ HIS REPLY ☐ HER REPLY

Has anyone ever given you a hard time about your ability? Who was it?

☐ HER REPLY ☐ HIS REPLY

☐ HIS REPLY ☐ HER REPLY

What was the best moment of today?

☐ HER REPLY ☐ HIS REPLY

☐ HIS REPLY ☐ HER REPLY

What do you think about when you wake up?

☐ HER REPLY ☐ HIS REPLY

☐ HIS REPLY ☐ HER REPLY

Which is more important to you, to get out there and keep walking, or to spend so much time on the phone with people who hate you that you're disconnected from your life?

☐ HER REPLY ☐ HIS REPLY   ☐ HIS REPLY ☐ HER REPLY

What are some of the most interesting places to work?

☐ HER REPLY ☐ HIS REPLY   ☐ HIS REPLY ☐ HER REPLY

Have you tried meditation before? Why?

☐ HER REPLY ☐ HIS REPLY

☐ HIS REPLY ☐ HER REPLY

If you could go back in time to the day you were born, how would it happen?

☐ HER REPLY ☐ HIS REPLY

☐ HIS REPLY ☐ HER REPLY

What do you think makes you smile?

☐ HER REPLY ☐ HIS REPLY

☐ HIS REPLY ☐ HER REPLY

If you had to choose one thing you could never lose, what would it be?

☐ HER REPLY ☐ HIS REPLY

☐ HIS REPLY ☐ HER REPLY

What's the strangest thing you've done while you were drunk?

□ HER REPLY □ HIS REPLY   □ HIS REPLY □ HER REPLY

Would you rather be a big fish in a little pond or a little fish in a big pond?

□ HER REPLY □ HIS REPLY   □ HIS REPLY □ HER REPLY

What you hope people will remember about you?

☐ HER REPLY ☐ HIS REPLY   ☐ HIS REPLY ☐ HER REPLY

If you could be famous for one day, what do you want to be famous for?

☐ HER REPLY ☐ HIS REPLY   ☐ HIS REPLY ☐ HER REPLY

What is the worst thing about a video game that you have never played?

☐ HER REPLY ☐ HIS REPLY   ☐ HIS REPLY ☐ HER REPLY

What do you wish to achieve in society?

☐ HER REPLY ☐ HIS REPLY   ☐ HIS REPLY ☐ HER REPLY

List of things that I want to see

☐ HER REPLY ☐ HIS REPLY

☐ HIS REPLY ☐ HER REPLY

Have you ever made some ethical choices in life? What did you do?

☐ HER REPLY ☐ HIS REPLY

☐ HIS REPLY ☐ HER REPLY

Which of your family's animals would you be?

☐ HER REPLY ☐ HIS REPLY

☐ HIS REPLY ☐ HER REPLY

What is the best thing that's happened in your life this year?

☐ HER REPLY ☐ HIS REPLY

☐ HIS REPLY ☐ HER REPLY

If you could tell your boss what you really want to do in your job, what would it be?

☐ HER REPLY ☐ HIS REPLY

☐ HIS REPLY ☐ HER REPLY

Do you like being alone? Why?

☐ HER REPLY ☐ HIS REPLY

☐ HIS REPLY ☐ HER REPLY

What would you say was the most memorable moment for you?

□ HER REPLY □ HIS REPLY

□ HIS REPLY □ HER REPLY

What it is important to be happy?

□ HER REPLY □ HIS REPLY

□ HIS REPLY □ HER REPLY

How would you describe the feeling of being viewed as a loser?

☐ HER REPLY ☐ HIS REPLY

☐ HIS REPLY ☐ HER REPLY

What is one thing you do not want to bring with you to a new place?

☐ HER REPLY ☐ HIS REPLY

☐ HIS REPLY ☐ HER REPLY

What's your favorite animal?

☐ HER REPLY ☐ HIS REPLY   ☐ HIS REPLY ☐ HER REPLY

What is it that you believe in?

☐ HER REPLY ☐ HIS REPLY   ☐ HIS REPLY ☐ HER REPLY

What is your most treasured memory?

☐ HER REPLY ☐ HIS REPLY

☐ HIS REPLY ☐ HER REPLY

What is the first step you take to realize your goals?

☐ HER REPLY ☐ HIS REPLY

☐ HIS REPLY ☐ HER REPLY

Say something about why it is important that you have this type of relationship.

☐ HER REPLY ☐ HIS REPLY

☐ HIS REPLY ☐ HER REPLY

What is true love?

☐ HER REPLY ☐ HIS REPLY

☐ HIS REPLY ☐ HER REPLY

How do you deal with someone who thinks you're the big fish in the pond?

☐ HER REPLY   ☐ HIS REPLY   ☐ HIS REPLY   ☐ HER REPLY

What is the one thing you can do to help you survive?

☐ HER REPLY   ☐ HIS REPLY   ☐ HIS REPLY   ☐ HER REPLY

If you were able to choose one thing from your parents' past that you're most thankful you got to live through, what would it be and why?

☐ HER REPLY ☐ HIS REPLY

☐ HIS REPLY ☐ HER REPLY

If you could travel anywhere in the world, where would it be?

☐ HER REPLY ☐ HIS REPLY

☐ HIS REPLY ☐ HER REPLY

How do you deal with non-paying customers?

☐ HER REPLY ☐ HIS REPLY

☐ HIS REPLY ☐ HER REPLY

How would you describe the feeling of being hard at work?

☐ HER REPLY ☐ HIS REPLY

☐ HIS REPLY ☐ HER REPLY

What is it that's preventing you from seeing the truth?

☐ HER REPLY ☐ HIS REPLY   ☐ HIS REPLY ☐ HER REPLY

If you found a magic lamp what 3 wishes would you ask the Genie for? What would each mean to you?

☐ HER REPLY ☐ HIS REPLY   ☐ HIS REPLY ☐ HER REPLY

What is the worst thing about a movie that you have never seen?

☐ HER REPLY   ☐ HIS REPLY

____
____
____
____
____
____
____
____
____

☐ HIS REPLY   ☐ HER REPLY

____
____
____
____
____
____
____
____
____

What do you enjoy doing the most?

☐ HER REPLY   ☐ HIS REPLY

____
____
____
____
____
____

☐ HIS REPLY   ☐ HER REPLY

____
____
____
____
____
____

Describe how to brush your teeth

☐ HER REPLY ☐ HIS REPLY

☐ HIS REPLY ☐ HER REPLY

What would you do for a dollar?

☐ HER REPLY ☐ HIS REPLY

☐ HIS REPLY ☐ HER REPLY

What makes you feel brave?

☐ HER REPLY ☐ HIS REPLY

☐ HIS REPLY ☐ HER REPLY

If you could make one game in the future, which one would it be?

☐ HER REPLY ☐ HIS REPLY

☐ HIS REPLY ☐ HER REPLY

What is the real-world value of what we are doing?

☐ HER REPLY ☐ HIS REPLY   ☐ HIS REPLY ☐ HER REPLY

What is one thing your superfans most want for you?

☐ HER REPLY ☐ HIS REPLY   ☐ HIS REPLY ☐ HER REPLY

☐ HER REPLY ☐ HIS REPLY   ☐ HIS REPLY ☐ HER REPLY

_______________________________   _______________________________
_______________________________   _______________________________
_______________________________   _______________________________
_______________________________   _______________________________
_______________________________   _______________________________
_______________________________   _______________________________
_______________________________   _______________________________
_______________________________   _______________________________

☐ HER REPLY ☐ HIS REPLY   ☐ HIS REPLY ☐ HER REPLY

_______________________________   _______________________________
_______________________________   _______________________________
_______________________________   _______________________________
_______________________________   _______________________________
_______________________________   _______________________________
_______________________________   _______________________________
_______________________________   _______________________________
_______________________________   _______________________________

What is your biggest goal for the future?

☐ HER REPLY ☐ HIS REPLY

☐ HIS REPLY ☐ HER REPLY

How do you think your work will help other people?

☐ HER REPLY ☐ HIS REPLY

☐ HIS REPLY ☐ HER REPLY

If you knew you would loose ever possession you own but one, what would you keep?

☐ HER REPLY ☐ HIS REPLY   ☐ HIS REPLY ☐ HER REPLY

List of things that have happened that you do want to get straight but keep deciding against

☐ HER REPLY ☐ HIS REPLY   ☐ HIS REPLY ☐ HER REPLY

Describe something you feel most passionate about to a complete stranger

☐ HER REPLY ☐ HIS REPLY

☐ HIS REPLY ☐ HER REPLY

How soon can you start?

☐ HER REPLY ☐ HIS REPLY

☐ HIS REPLY ☐ HER REPLY

When do you first feel like quitting?

☐ HER REPLY ☐ HIS REPLY

____

☐ HIS REPLY ☐ HER REPLY

____

Would you rather be here today (where you are right now) or would you rather be here 20 years from now?

☐ HER REPLY ☐ HIS REPLY

____

☐ HIS REPLY ☐ HER REPLY

____

What would you like to have?

☐ HER REPLY ☐ HIS REPLY　　　　　☐ HIS REPLY ☐ HER REPLY

Why do you have to have one for the sake of having one?

☐ HER REPLY ☐ HIS REPLY　　　　　☐ HIS REPLY ☐ HER REPLY

If you could be completely defined by one word or concept, what would it be and why?

☐ HER REPLY ☐ HIS REPLY

____
____
____
____
____
____
____

☐ HIS REPLY ☐ HER REPLY

____
____
____
____
____
____
____

What's on your bucket list?

☐ HER REPLY ☐ HIS REPLY

____
____
____
____
____
____
____

☐ HIS REPLY ☐ HER REPLY

____
____
____
____
____
____
____

Do you think it's okay to keep secrets? Why?

☐ HER REPLY ☐ HIS REPLY   ☐ HIS REPLY ☐ HER REPLY

What is one thing you have in common with your dog?

☐ HER REPLY ☐ HIS REPLY   ☐ HIS REPLY ☐ HER REPLY

List of things that you might want to create

☐ HER REPLY ☐ HIS REPLY

____

☐ HIS REPLY ☐ HER REPLY

____

How do you actually view yourself?

☐ HER REPLY ☐ HIS REPLY

____

☐ HIS REPLY ☐ HER REPLY

____

When you were a kid, what did you want to be when you grew up?

☐ HER REPLY ☐ HIS REPLY

☐ HIS REPLY ☐ HER REPLY

What is the best gift you have received so far this year?

☐ HER REPLY ☐ HIS REPLY

☐ HIS REPLY ☐ HER REPLY

Must you feel that all your efforts are worth nothing? Why or why not?

☐ HER REPLY   ☐ HIS REPLY

☐ HIS REPLY   ☐ HER REPLY

What would you invent to make life better?

☐ HER REPLY   ☐ HIS REPLY

☐ HIS REPLY   ☐ HER REPLY

Describe your perfect happiness

□ HER REPLY □ HIS REPLY

□ HIS REPLY □ HER REPLY

Describe how weather affects your commute to school.

□ HER REPLY □ HIS REPLY

□ HIS REPLY □ HER REPLY

What's your first reaction when you see a new species?

☐ HER REPLY ☐ HIS REPLY   ☐ HIS REPLY ☐ HER REPLY

List of things that came to your mind first

☐ HER REPLY ☐ HIS REPLY   ☐ HIS REPLY ☐ HER REPLY

Why do you want to be a good person?

☐ HER REPLY ☐ HIS REPLY   ☐ HIS REPLY ☐ HER REPLY

How do you deal with people who don't understand that you care about them?

☐ HER REPLY ☐ HIS REPLY   ☐ HIS REPLY ☐ HER REPLY

What does it mean for you to have a passion?

☐ HER REPLY ☐ HIS REPLY

☐ HIS REPLY ☐ HER REPLY

List of things iced

☐ HER REPLY ☐ HIS REPLY

☐ HIS REPLY ☐ HER REPLY

What is your favorite color combination?

□ HER REPLY □ HIS REPLY

□ HIS REPLY □ HER REPLY

What would be your craziest date idea?

□ HER REPLY □ HIS REPLY

□ HIS REPLY □ HER REPLY

What is the one most difficult thing you have to do to succeed?

☐ HER REPLY   ☐ HIS REPLY   ☐ HIS REPLY   ☐ HER REPLY

How do you deal with negative feedback?

☐ HER REPLY   ☐ HIS REPLY   ☐ HIS REPLY   ☐ HER REPLY

Have you lived a double life?

☐ HER REPLY ☐ HIS REPLY

☐ HIS REPLY ☐ HER REPLY

Favorite movie set in the '80s?

☐ HER REPLY ☐ HIS REPLY

☐ HIS REPLY ☐ HER REPLY

How do you deal with anxiety when you're not trying to deal with it?

☐ HER REPLY ☐ HIS REPLY

☐ HIS REPLY ☐ HER REPLY

What will you do if you find out there is nothing?

☐ HER REPLY ☐ HIS REPLY

☐ HIS REPLY ☐ HER REPLY

How are you different from who you once were?

☐ HER REPLY ☐ HIS REPLY

☐ HIS REPLY ☐ HER REPLY

If you could tell your life story to another person, what would that story be? Will it be good or bad?

☐ HER REPLY ☐ HIS REPLY

☐ HIS REPLY ☐ HER REPLY

Are you a person of pleasure or want power or control? Why?

☐ HER REPLY ☐ HIS REPLY

____
____
____
____
____
____
____
____
____

☐ HIS REPLY ☐ HER REPLY

____
____
____
____
____
____
____
____
____

What good is going to come of it?

☐ HER REPLY ☐ HIS REPLY

____
____
____
____
____
____
____

☐ HIS REPLY ☐ HER REPLY

____
____
____
____
____
____
____

How would you describe the feeling of being overwhelmed by experience?

☐ HER REPLY ☐ HIS REPLY   ☐ HIS REPLY ☐ HER REPLY

Do you have any other hobbies? Why? Why not?

☐ HER REPLY ☐ HIS REPLY   ☐ HIS REPLY ☐ HER REPLY

If you could be any color for another season then, what color would you choose?

☐ HER REPLY ☐ HIS REPLY   ☐ HIS REPLY ☐ HER REPLY

You're out of a job and need some extra money. Who do you call to help you get it?

☐ HER REPLY ☐ HIS REPLY   ☐ HIS REPLY ☐ HER REPLY

How would you describe the feeling of being cheated on?

☐ HER REPLY ☐ HIS REPLY

☐ HIS REPLY ☐ HER REPLY

What is the one thing you have learned about yourself that helped you gain confidence?

☐ HER REPLY ☐ HIS REPLY

☐ HIS REPLY ☐ HER REPLY

What is your favorite movie to watch?

☐ HER REPLY ☐ HIS REPLY

☐ HIS REPLY ☐ HER REPLY

List of things that are beyond comprehension and too scary for me

☐ HER REPLY ☐ HIS REPLY

☐ HIS REPLY ☐ HER REPLY

What scares you the most?

☐ HER REPLY ☐ HIS REPLY   ☐ HIS REPLY ☐ HER REPLY

________________________________   ________________________________
________________________________   ________________________________
________________________________   ________________________________
________________________________   ________________________________
________________________________   ________________________________
________________________________   ________________________________
________________________________   ________________________________

What are the three main problems with your body?

☐ HER REPLY ☐ HIS REPLY   ☐ HIS REPLY ☐ HER REPLY

________________________________   ________________________________
________________________________   ________________________________
________________________________   ________________________________
________________________________   ________________________________
________________________________   ________________________________
________________________________   ________________________________
________________________________   ________________________________

Are you religious or spiritual? Why?

☐ HER REPLY ☐ HIS REPLY ☐ HIS REPLY ☐ HER REPLY

If you had to choose one thing about yourself or someone you know that you think will change the way they view the world, what would it be?

☐ HER REPLY ☐ HIS REPLY ☐ HIS REPLY ☐ HER REPLY

How do you deal with bad things?

☐ HER REPLY ☐ HIS REPLY

☐ HIS REPLY ☐ HER REPLY

What's a good way to tell if someone is crazy?

☐ HER REPLY ☐ HIS REPLY

☐ HIS REPLY ☐ HER REPLY

How does your child feel when she's afraid?

□ HER REPLY □ HIS REPLY

□ HIS REPLY □ HER REPLY

How do you find your place in life?

□ HER REPLY □ HIS REPLY

□ HIS REPLY □ HER REPLY

What was the most frightening part about what happened in your last three weeks?

☐ HER REPLY ☐ HIS REPLY

☐ HIS REPLY ☐ HER REPLY

What's the most thing you don't like about yourself?

☐ HER REPLY ☐ HIS REPLY

☐ HIS REPLY ☐ HER REPLY

What's your favorite type of ice cream?

☐ HER REPLY ☐ HIS REPLY

☐ HIS REPLY ☐ HER REPLY

List of things that do not escape you

☐ HER REPLY ☐ HIS REPLY

☐ HIS REPLY ☐ HER REPLY

What does a good relationship look like between you and the people you care about?

☐ HER REPLY ☐ HIS REPLY

☐ HIS REPLY ☐ HER REPLY

What do you need to know now?

☐ HER REPLY ☐ HIS REPLY

☐ HIS REPLY ☐ HER REPLY

Which would you choose between having the greatest possible access to money or having the greatest possible access to women? Why?

☐ HER REPLY ☐ HIS REPLY

☐ HIS REPLY ☐ HER REPLY

What happened last night?

☐ HER REPLY ☐ HIS REPLY

☐ HIS REPLY ☐ HER REPLY

If you could choose the three words that will define the next decade, what would they be?

☐ HER REPLY ☐ HIS REPLY

☐ HIS REPLY ☐ HER REPLY

What is a principle or ideal that you would like to pass on to the next generation?

☐ HER REPLY ☐ HIS REPLY

☐ HIS REPLY ☐ HER REPLY

What is most important to you to help you make decisions?

☐ HER REPLY ☐ HIS REPLY

☐ HIS REPLY ☐ HER REPLY

Will you take the steps to make it disappear? Why?

☐ HER REPLY ☐ HIS REPLY

☐ HIS REPLY ☐ HER REPLY

When was the first time you went into the ocean and saw
sharks?

☐ HER REPLY ☐ HIS REPLY   ☐ HIS REPLY ☐ HER REPLY

What is one thing you have in common with your favorite
food?

☐ HER REPLY ☐ HIS REPLY   ☐ HIS REPLY ☐ HER REPLY

How have your thoughts on things changed over the time you've had time to think of alternatives?

☐ HER REPLY ☐ HIS REPLY

☐ HIS REPLY ☐ HER REPLY

Which is more important to you, to look like a brainiac or to look good? Why?

☐ HER REPLY ☐ HIS REPLY

☐ HIS REPLY ☐ HER REPLY

Have you ever cheated on someone with someone else?

☐ HER REPLY ☐ HIS REPLY   ☐ HIS REPLY ☐ HER REPLY

List of things that you want to try more

☐ HER REPLY ☐ HIS REPLY   ☐ HIS REPLY ☐ HER REPLY

What would you wish you had been born with?

☐ HER REPLY　☐ HIS REPLY

☐ HIS REPLY　☐ HER REPLY

How would you describe the feeling of being part of a people that you may have sometimes been frightened of?

☐ HER REPLY　☐ HIS REPLY

☐ HIS REPLY　☐ HER REPLY

What does your child like to do when he/she's angry?

☐ HER REPLY ☐ HIS REPLY

☐ HIS REPLY ☐ HER REPLY

If you could go to your favorite place, describe through your imagination on how do you get there?

☐ HER REPLY ☐ HIS REPLY

☐ HIS REPLY ☐ HER REPLY

If you had to choose one thing to improve upon, what would you choose?

☐ HER REPLY   ☐ HIS REPLY

☐ HIS REPLY   ☐ HER REPLY

What are your feelings of love and attachment when you're young?

☐ HER REPLY   ☐ HIS REPLY

☐ HIS REPLY   ☐ HER REPLY

What's your favorite thing to do in the evenings?

☐ HER REPLY ☐ HIS REPLY

☐ HIS REPLY ☐ HER REPLY

What is your favorite hobby and why?

☐ HER REPLY ☐ HIS REPLY

☐ HIS REPLY ☐ HER REPLY

What do you wish you could tell someone that you haven't told anybody elese?

☐ HER REPLY ☐ HIS REPLY ☐ HIS REPLY ☐ HER REPLY

How would you describe the feeling of being in prison?

☐ HER REPLY ☐ HIS REPLY ☐ HIS REPLY ☐ HER REPLY

What would you change to give yourself more fun?

☐ HER REPLY ☐ HIS REPLY

☐ HIS REPLY ☐ HER REPLY

How would you feel if you found out the last person you talked to had cancer?

☐ HER REPLY ☐ HIS REPLY

☐ HIS REPLY ☐ HER REPLY

What causes you to feel so bad about yourself?

☐ HER REPLY ☐ HIS REPLY

____
____
____
____
____
____
____
____

☐ HIS REPLY ☐ HER REPLY

____
____
____
____
____
____
____
____

Do you have any other tips for parents?

☐ HER REPLY ☐ HIS REPLY

____
____
____
____
____
____
____

☐ HIS REPLY ☐ HER REPLY

____
____
____
____
____
____
____

What is the most important thing you can give your future self?

☐ HER REPLY ☐ HIS REPLY   ☐ HIS REPLY ☐ HER REPLY

Who will be the villain in your story?

☐ HER REPLY ☐ HIS REPLY   ☐ HIS REPLY ☐ HER REPLY

List of things that have a chance of happening and people believe in

☐ HER REPLY ☐ HIS REPLY   ☐ HIS REPLY ☐ HER REPLY

Will you have anything similar in mind?

☐ HER REPLY ☐ HIS REPLY   ☐ HIS REPLY ☐ HER REPLY

What is the one thing you can see that doesn't matter?

☐ HER REPLY ☐ HIS REPLY

☐ HIS REPLY ☐ HER REPLY

What makes you feel so bad?

☐ HER REPLY ☐ HIS REPLY

☐ HIS REPLY ☐ HER REPLY

List of things that might have happened

☐ HER REPLY ☐ HIS REPLY

____

☐ HIS REPLY ☐ HER REPLY

____

Would that be a good place to start? Why?

☐ HER REPLY ☐ HIS REPLY

____

☐ HIS REPLY ☐ HER REPLY

____

What would make you smile?

☐ HER REPLY ☐ HIS REPLY

☐ HIS REPLY ☐ HER REPLY

If you could be someone else who would that be and why?

☐ HER REPLY ☐ HIS REPLY

☐ HIS REPLY ☐ HER REPLY

How many days have you been on vacation in the last two years?

☐ HER REPLY ☐ HIS REPLY   ☐ HIS REPLY ☐ HER REPLY

What is the one thing which you must never do?

☐ HER REPLY ☐ HIS REPLY   ☐ HIS REPLY ☐ HER REPLY

What would you prefer for your future?

☐ HER REPLY ☐ HIS REPLY   ☐ HIS REPLY ☐ HER REPLY

Do you have a particular fantasy of somebody else? Who is it?

☐ HER REPLY ☐ HIS REPLY   ☐ HIS REPLY ☐ HER REPLY

At what point did you realize you were doing the right thing?

☐ HER REPLY ☐ HIS REPLY   ☐ HIS REPLY ☐ HER REPLY

What is one thing that you want more people to know about your life?

☐ HER REPLY ☐ HIS REPLY   ☐ HIS REPLY ☐ HER REPLY

Why are you late again?

☐ HER REPLY ☐ HIS REPLY

☐ HIS REPLY ☐ HER REPLY

What if you were given the chance to travel the world, where would you go?

☐ HER REPLY ☐ HIS REPLY

☐ HIS REPLY ☐ HER REPLY

☐ HER REPLY ☐ HIS REPLY

☐ HIS REPLY ☐ HER REPLY

☐ HER REPLY ☐ HIS REPLY

☐ HIS REPLY ☐ HER REPLY

Would you rather be a woman or a man?

☐ HER REPLY ☐ HIS REPLY

☐ HIS REPLY ☐ HER REPLY

How do you feel about using humans in medical research?

☐ HER REPLY ☐ HIS REPLY

☐ HIS REPLY ☐ HER REPLY

If you could change the entire world, what would you change?

☐ HER REPLY ☐ HIS REPLY

☐ HIS REPLY ☐ HER REPLY

I love you. I love you not because… [continue the sentence]

☐ HER REPLY ☐ HIS REPLY

☐ HIS REPLY ☐ HER REPLY

Do you ever feel afraid? Why?

☐ HER REPLY ☐ HIS REPLY

☐ HIS REPLY ☐ HER REPLY

What would you do if you dropped the cookie jar and it broke?

☐ HER REPLY ☐ HIS REPLY

☐ HIS REPLY ☐ HER REPLY

What can you say as a kid but can't as an adult?

☐ HER REPLY ☐ HIS REPLY

☐ HIS REPLY ☐ HER REPLY

What is a joke you played on someone?

☐ HER REPLY ☐ HIS REPLY

☐ HIS REPLY ☐ HER REPLY

What is the one thing you will never change about you?

☐ HER REPLY   ☐ HIS REPLY

☐ HIS REPLY   ☐ HER REPLY

When you meet someone you haven't seen in a long time, you are often surprised by how much they have changed. Describe a time when this happened to you.

☐ HER REPLY   ☐ HIS REPLY

☐ HIS REPLY   ☐ HER REPLY

What legacy do you want to leave the world?

☐ HER REPLY ☐ HIS REPLY

☐ HIS REPLY ☐ HER REPLY

Describe an experience you had that was so strange others might think you made it up.

☐ HER REPLY ☐ HIS REPLY

☐ HIS REPLY ☐ HER REPLY

Would you be able to tell if time had been altered in some way? How?

☐ HER REPLY   ☐ HIS REPLY

☐ HIS REPLY   ☐ HER REPLY

What is the most significant area of improvement in your life?

☐ HER REPLY   ☐ HIS REPLY

☐ HIS REPLY   ☐ HER REPLY